D1609676

Belongs to:

_____

_____

_____

my prayer journal

my prayer journal

journal

a daily inspirational journal

world
PUBLISHING
SINCE 1928

my prayer journal

THE LORD'S PRAYER

After this manner therefore pray ye:
Our Father which art in heaven,
Hallowed be thy name.
Thy kingdom come, Thy will be
done on earth, as it is in heaven.
Give us this day our daily bread.
And forgive us our debts, as we
forgive our debtors.
And lead us not into temptation, but
deliver us from evil:
For thine is the kingdom, and the
power, and the glory, for ever. Amen.

—Matthew 6:9-13 KJV

It is an old custom of the servants of God to have some little prayer ready and to be frequently darting them up to Heaven during the day, lifting their minds to God out of the mire of this world. He who adopts this plan will get great fruits with little pains.

—**Philip Neri**

*While Jesus lived on earth,
he prayed to God and asked God for help.
He prayed with loud cries and tears to the
One who could save him from death, and
his prayer was heard because he trusted God.*
—**Hebrews 5:7** NCV

January

Prayer is a dove, the bird of the Holy Spirit, which brings the olive branch and wins peace for humankind.

—William Peraldus

Ask, and it will be given to you; seek, and you will find; knock, and it will be opened to you. For everyone who asks receives, and he who seeks finds, and to him who knocks it will be opened.

—Matthew 7:7-8

If you feel stuck, bring your whole self to Christ, not just the problem, but you. Ask God to change your heart. Commit yourself to pray to that end. It's God's heart to give good gifts to His children.

—**Sheila Walsh**

Build yourself a cell in your heart and retire there to pray.

—Catherine of Siena

In prayer, it is better to have a heart without words, than words without a heart.

—John Bunyan

Take ye heed, watch and pray: for ye know not when the time is.
—Mark 13:33 KJV

There are many things that are essential to arriving at true peace of mind, and one of the most important is faith, which cannot be acquired without prayer.

—John Wooden

Fifteen Reasons to Pray

1. To seek the face of the Lord and know him better (Ps. 27.8)
2. To get your eyes off your problems and onto the Lord (Ps. 121.1)
3. To speak to God (1 Peter 3:12)
4. To unburden your heart (Ps. 142:1–2)
5. To make your requests known to God (Matt. 21:22)
6. To hear God (Prov. 8:34)
7. To be free of suffering (James 5:13)
8. To resist temptation (Matt. 26:41)
9. To be rescued from distress (Ps. 107:19)
10. To receive God's reward (Matt. 6:6)
11. To withstand evil (Eph. 6:13)
12. To have joy (Eph. 6:13)
13. To get close to God (Is. 64:7)
14. To be healed emotionally (James 5:13)
15. To have peace (Phil. 4:6–7)

—Stormie Omartian, *Praying God's Will for Your Life*

Now, O my God, I pray, let Your eyes be open and Your ears attentive to the prayer offered in this place.
—2 Chronicles 6:40 NASB

To be a Christian without prayer is no more possible than being alive without breathing.

—Martin Luther

And pray in the Spirit on all occasions with all kinds of prayers and requests. With this in mind, be alert and always keep on praying for all the saints.
—Ephesians 6:18 NIV

Prayer is a shield to the soul,
a sacrifice to God, and a scourge to Satan.

—John Bunyan

A good prayer, though often used, is still fresh and fair in the eyes and ears of heaven.

—Thomas Fuller

We are urged to pray for one another but that does not mean that we abdicate our individual commitment to pray for ourselves.

—Sheila Walsh

Do not worry about anything, but pray and ask God for every thing you need, always giving thanks.
—Philippians 4:6 NCV

13 January

The soul must be kept peaceful during prayer and end prayer in peace.

—Jean Pierre de Caussade

Be joyful in hope, patient in
affliction, faithful in prayer
—Romans 12:12 NIV

As soon as we are with God in faith and in love, we are in prayer.

—**François Fénelon**

There is a place where thou canst touch the eyes
Of blinded men to instant, perfect sight;
There is a place where thou canst say, "Arise"
To dying captives, bound in chains of night;
There is a place where thou canst reach the store
Of hoarded gold and free it for the Lord;
There is a place--upon some distant shore--
Where thou canst send the worker and the Word.
Where is that secret place--dost thou ask, "Where?"
O soul, it is the secret place of prayer!

—Alfred, Lord Tennyson

*Prayer is the application of the heart to God, and
the internal exercise of love.*

—Madame Jeanne Guyon

*Now therefore, I pray, if I have
found grace in Your sight, show
me now Your way, that I may
know You and that I may find
grace in Your sight.*
—Exodus 33:13

He who has learned to pray has learned the greatest secret of a holy and happy life.

—William Law

Praise the LORD and pray in his name! Tell everyone what he has done.
—1 Chronicles 16:8 CEV

Don't let controversy hurt your soul. Live near to God by prayer. Just fall down at His feet and open your very soul before Him, and throw yourself right into His arms.

—**Catherine Booth**

Prayer is the guide to perfection, and delivers us from every vice and gives us every virtue; for the one way to become perfect is to walk in the presence of God.

—Madame Jeanne Guyon

Confess your faults one to another, and pray one for another, that ye may be healed. The effectual fervent prayer of a righteous man availeth much.

—James 5:16 KJV

A prayer in its simplest definition is merely a wish turned Godward.

—Phillips Brooks

The longer one prays, the better it goes.

—John Chapman

*Moreover, as for me, far be it from
me that I should sin against the Lord
by ceasing to pray for you, but I will
instruct you in the good and right way.*
—1 Samuel 12:23

It matters little what form of prayer we adopt . . . or how many words we use. What matters is the faith which lays hold on God, knowing that He knows our needs before we even ask Him. That is what gives Christian prayer its boundless confidence and its joyous certainty. We simply make petitions and requests to One who has the heart of a Father.

—Dietrich Bonhoeffer

Prayer is and remains always a native and deep impulse of the soul of man.

—Thomas Carlyle

Prayer is the effort to live in the spirit of the whole.

—Samuel Taylor Coleridge

*Cast your cares on the Lord and He will
sustain you.*
—Psalm 55:22 NIV

Jesus' delay in answering our prayers is never due to indifference or preoccupation with other things or an inability to act. His delay has a purpose.

—Anne Graham Lotz

Prayer should be the key of the day and the lock of the night.

—**Thomas Fuller**

*Call to me and I will answer you
and tell you great and unsearchable
things you do not know.*
—**Jeremiah 33:3**

Do not turn to prayer hoping to enjoy spiritual delights; rather come to prayer totally content to receive nothing or to receive great blessing from God's hand, whichever should be your heavenly Father's will for you at that time.

—Madame Jeanne Guyon

Hear my cry, O God;
Attend to my prayer.
—Psalm 61:1

There is nothing that makes us love a man so much as praying for him.

—William Law

THE SERENITY PRAYER

God grant me the serenity
to accept the things I cannot change;
courage to change the things I can;
and wisdom to know the difference.
Living one day at a time;
Enjoying one moment at a time;
Accepting hardships as the pathway to peace;
Taking, as He did, this sinful world
as it is, not as I would have it;
Trusting that He will make all things right
if I surrender to His Will;
That I may be reasonably happy in this life
and supremely happy with Him
Forever in the next.
Amen.

—Reinhold Niebuhr

Lord, may I be directed what to do and what to leave undone.

—Elizabeth Fry

Their voice was heard and their prayer came His holy dwelling place, to heaven.
—2 Chronicles 30:27 NASB

Help us, this and every day, to live more nearly as we pray.

—John Keble

Men ought always to pray, and not to faint.
        —Luke 18:1 KJV

Prayer does not change God, but it changes him who prays.

—Søren Kierkegaard

February

I will thank God for the pleasures given me through my senses, for the glory of the thunder, for the mystery of music, the singing of the birds and the laughter of children . . . Truly, O Lord, the earth is full of thy riches.

—Edward King

Do not attempt to assess the quality of your prayer.
God alone can judge its value.

—Macarius of Optino

While Jesus lived on earth, he prayed to God
and asked God for help. He prayed with loud
cries and tears to the One who could save
him from death, and his prayer was heard
because he trusted God.
—Hebrews 5:7 NCV

Prayer isn't some kind of requirement for believers. It is a privilege!

—**Christa Kinde**

If we pray for anything according to the will of God, we already have what we pray for the moment we ask it. We do not know exactly when it will arrive; but we have learned to know God through the Spirit of God; and have learned to leave this in His hands; and to live just as happily whether the answer arrives immediately or later.

—O. Hallesby

*Hannah prayed: You make me strong and happy, L*ORD*. You rescued me. Now I can be glad and laugh at my enemies.*
—1 Samuel 2:1 CEV

February

If I could hear Christ praying for me in the next room, I would not fear a million enemies. Yet distance makes no difference. He is praying for me.

—**Robert Murray M'Cheyne**

Does God care about the little things in our lives?
You better believe it. If it matters to you, it matters to Him.

—Max Lucado

Yet regard the prayer of Your servant and his
supplication, O LORD my God, and listen to
the cry and the prayer which Your servant is
praying before You today.
—1 Kings 8:28

The Lord's Prayer may be committed to memory quickly, but it is slowly learnt by heart.

—Frederick Denison Maurice

Please answer my prayer and the prayer of your other servants who gladly honor your name. . . . .
—Nehemiah 1:11 CEV

Strive never to pray against anyone.

—**Evagrius of Pontus**

Truly we have learned a great lesson when we have learned that 'saying prayers' is not praying!

—John Charles Ryle

Thank God every morning when you get up that you have something to do which must be done whether you like it or not. Being forced to work, and forced to do your best, will breed in you temperance, self-control, diligence, strength of will, content, and a hundred other virtues which the idle will never know.

—Charles Kingsley

Be sure to obey all my instructions. And remember, never pray to or swear by any other gods. Do not even mention their names.
—Exodus 23:13 NLT

DID YOU THINK TO PRAY?

Ere you left your room this morning,
Did you think to pray?
In the name of Christ our Savior,
Did you sue for loving favor,
As a shield today?

When you met with great temptation,
Did you think to pray?
By His dying love and merit,
Did you claim the Holy Spirit
As your guide and stay?

When your heart was filled with anger,
Did you think to pray?
Did you plead for grace, my brother,
That you might forgive another
Who had crossed your way?

When sore trials came upon you,
Did you think to pray?
When your soul was bowed in sorrow,
Balm of Gilead did you borrow
At the gates of day?

O how praying rests the weary!
Prayer will change the night to day;
So when life seems dark and dreary,
Don't forget to pray.

—Mary A. Kidder

Depend on prayer; prayer is powerful.

—John Charles Ryle

I sought the LORD, and He heard me, And delivered me from all my fears.
—**Psalm 34:4**

I used to ask God to help me. Then I asked if I might help Him. I ended up by asking Him to do His work through me.

—James Hudson Taylor

Prayer is the test of everything; prayer is also the source of everything; prayer is the driving force of everything; prayer is also the director of everything. If prayer is right, everything is right. For prayer will not allow anything to go wrong.

—Theophan the Recluse

And they continued steadfastly in the apostles' doctrine and fellowship, and in the breaking of bread, and in prayers.
—Acts 2:42

It is from prayer that the spirit's victory springs.

—Schillerbuch

And the LORD turned the captivity of Job, when he prayed for his friends: also the LORD gave Job twice as much as he had before.
—Job 42:10 KJV

Prayer is not overcoming God's reluctance;
it is laying hold of His highest willingness.

—**Richard Chevenix Trench**

Father, hear the prayer we offer; not for ease that prayer shall be, but for strength that we may ever, live our lives courageously.

—Maria Willis

He heeded their prayer, because they put their trust in Him.
—1 Chronicles 5:20

Prayer Partners with God

Have you ever faced a situation that was so overwhelming or so confusing you didn't even know how to pray about it? Have you ever been so overcome with grief or burdened by heartache you couldn't put your emotions into words—much less pray about them?

What a comfort these words should be: The Spirit helps us in our weakness. We do not know what we ought to pray, but the Spirit himself intercedes for us . . . in accordance with God's will" (Romans 8:26-27, NIV).

Think of it: Even when we don't know how to pray, the Spirit knows our needs, and He brings the deepest cries of our hearts before the throne of God. In ways we will never understand this side of eternity, God the Holy Spirit pleads for us before God the Father.

Turn to God in every situation—even when you don't feel like it. The Spirit is interceding for you, in accordance with God's will.

—Billy Graham, *Hope for Each Day*

February

Man knows mighty little, and may some day
learn enough of his own ignorance to fall down and pray.

—**Henry Brooks Adams**

Over the last few years I have discovered that what is most changed by prayer is the one who is praying.

—Sheila Walsh

If My people who are called by My name will humble themselves, and pray and seek My face, and turn from their wicked ways, then I will hear from heaven, and will forgive their sin and heal their land.
—2 Chronicles 7:14

Prayer is talking with God and telling Him you love Him, conversing with God about all the things that are important in life, both large and small, and being assured that He is listening.

—C. Neil Strait

While he was in distress he entreated the favour of the LORD his God and humbled himself greatly before the God of his ancestors. He prayed to him, and God received his entreaty, heard his plea, and restored him again to Jerusalem and to his kingdom. Then Manasseh knew that the LORD indeed was God.

—2 Chronicles 33:12-13 NRSV

Prayer, in the sense of union with God,
is the most crucifying thing there is.

—**John Chapman**

*We pray because we are made for prayer, and
God draws us out by breathing himself in.*

—Peter Taylor Forsyth

*Prayer is practical when it affects our outer conduct,
but still more when it affects our inner activity.*

—Maud D. Petre

*I do not pray for these alone, but
also for those who will believe in Me
through their word.*
—John 17:20

Of course, God's will must be the primary object of our prayers . . . and we must recognize prayer as an instrument of God's will. Therefore, we pray that God's will may be done throughout the world . . . and in intercessory prayer we bring people . . . from around the world . . . into the presence of God.

—Dietrich Bonhoeffer

When I pray, you answer me; you encourage me by giving me the strength I need.
—Psalm 138:3 NLT

We can be tired, weary and emotionally distraught, but after spending time alone with God, we find that He injects into our bodies energy, power, and strength.

—Charles Stanley

Near to losing heart? Are you overborne with labor?
Or worn out with worry? Or consumed with hopeless longings?
Then won't you take your Lord's advice? Don't try to keep the whole thing
pent up within your own heart. Share it with God. Tell him all
about it, yes, down to the last and absurdest annoying detail.

—**John Baillie**

The worst sin is prayerlessness.

—Peter Taylor Forsyth

God has seen how I never stop praying for you, while I serve him with all my heart and tell the good news about his Son.
—Romans 1:9 CEV

March

Prayer, Christian prayer, is the supreme weapon
in the struggle in which we are called to take part.

—Louis Bouyer

Pray confidently. But be careful what you pray for—because everything and anything is possible through the power of prayer.

—Barbara Johnson

You will make your prayer to Him, He will hear you, And you will pay your vows.
—Job 22:27

To pray is to sit openhanded before God

—Peter G. Van Breemen

He shall pray to God, and He will delight in him, He shall see His face with joy, For He restores to man His righteousness.
—Job 33:26

PRAY, PRAY

Pray, pray, when things go wrong,
And gloomy fears around you throng;
The loving God your voice will hear,
Look up to Him, He's always near.

Pray, pray, be calm and still,
Whatever comes must be His will;
His promises like buds unfold,
Naught that is good will He withhold.

Pray, pray till faith grows strong,
And in your heart rings heaven's song;
Till self shall die in pure desire,
And every thought to Him aspire.

Pray, pray though your eyes grow dim,
Go with your troubles straight to Him;
Pray, pray, for God understands;
Have faith, leaving all in His dear hands.

—Lizzie DeArmond

March

Prayer is my link to sanity, stability, and longevity.

—Patsy Clairmont

Pray as you can, and do not try to pray as you can't.

—John Chapman

*Give ear to my words, O LORD,
consider my meditation.
Hearken unto the voice of my cry,
my King, and my God: for unto thee
will I pray.
My voice shalt thou hear in the
morning, O LORD; in the morning
will I direct my prayer unto thee,
and will look up.*
—Psalm 5:1-3 KJV

March

Prayer is the core of our day. Take prayer out and the day would collapse.

—Amy Carmichael

There is something much greater than human action—prayer.

—Carlo Carretto

The Lord has heard my supplication;
the Lord accepts my prayer
—Psalm 6:9 NRSV

Discover the secret of praying Scripture, for God loves to be reminded of His word. He invites us to approach His throne boldly — on the basis of His word and through the shed blood of Jesus Christ — to obtain mercy and to find grace to help in time of need.

—Robert J. Morgan

Prayer is not work and work is not prayer.

—Joan Chittister

*Hear a just cause, O LORD, Attend to
my cry; Give ear to my prayer which is
not from deceitful lips.*
—Psalm 17:1

In the name of Jesus Christ, who was never in a hurry, we pray, O God, that You will slow us down, for we know that we live too fast. With all of eternity before us, make us take time to live—time to get acquainted with You, time to enjoy Your blessings, and time to each other.

—Peter Marshall

No matter what has happened to you or is happening in the world around you, God promises to protect you as you walk with Him. Pray that He will and trust Him to do so.

—Stormie Omartian

Yet the LORD will command his lovingkindness in the day time, and in the night his song shall be with me, and my prayer unto the God of my life.
—Psalm 42:8 KJV

We will not find God in our homes unless we stop and pray there.

—Margaret Hebblethwaite

Hear my prayer, O God; give ear to the words
of my mouth.
—Psalm 54:2 KJV

When you pray, you must yourself be silent. You do not pray to
have your own earthbound desires fulfilled, but you pray:
Thy will be done. It is not fitting to use God as an errand boy.
You yourself must be silent; let the prayer speak.

—Tito Colliander

Real power in prayer flows only when man's spirit touches God's spirit.

—**Catherine Marshall**

The more we receive in silent prayer,
the more we can give in active life.

—Malcolm Muggeridge

But certainly God has heard me; He has
attended to the voice of my prayer.
—Psalm 66:19

God puts a great deal more value on our prayers than we do.
He considers prayer to be a serious thing that can influence events
in this world—both events in our personal lives and
events in world history and current events.

—Robert J. Morgan

Let us then approach the throne
of grace with confidence, so that
we may receive mercy and find
grace to help us in our time of
need.

—Hebrews 4:16 NIV

THE PRAYING HANDS STORY

The famous "Study of Praying Hands" created in 1508 by Albrecht Dürer has a history as touching and beautiful as the artwork itself.

When the young Albrecht was studying art, he and Franz Knigstein, a friend and fellow art student worked as laborers to pay their tuition costs. Their long work hours left little time for art. Rather than having both of them fail at their art studies, they decided one should work while the other attended school.

Franz agreed to work as a laborer, while Albrecht gratefully pursued his art career—promising to return the favor once he became a successful artist. Much time passed as Albrecht developed his potential genius. Finally he returned to keep his promise to Franz, who was overjoyed at Albrecht's success. Soon Albrecht realized that the years of labor had been hard on Franz. His fingers had become too bent and twisted to manipulate a paintbrush. He could never become the artist he hoped to be, nor could Albrecht ever fulfill his promise of repayment.

One night, as Franz knelt in prayer, Albrecht sorrowfully sketched the crippled hands of the friend who had made his success possible. Albrecht Dürer's beautiful artwork is a tribute to the spirit of love and sacrifice to which Franz Knigstein's life was testimony.

—Unknown

The man of prayer finds his happiness in
continually creating, searching, being with Christ.

—Roger of Taizé

I believe we get an answer to our prayers when we are willing to obey what is implicit in that answer. I believe that we get a vision of God when we are willing to accept what that vision does to us.

—Elsie Chamberlain

Evening and morning and at noon I will pray, and cry aloud, And He shall hear my voice.
—Psalm 55:17 KJV

Prayer is an exercise of the spirit, as thought is of the mind.

—Mary F. Smith

He shall regard the prayer of the destitute,
And shall not despise their prayer.
—Psalm 102:17 NRSV

Prayer is not us trying to grab hold of God.
Prayer is to recognize God coming to us.

—Stephen Verney

One of the first things for which we have to pray is a true insight into our condition.

—Oliver Wyon

Anything large enough for a wish to light upon,
is large enough to hang a prayer upon.

—George MacDonald

For the eyes of the LORD are on the righteous,
And His ears are open to their prayers; But
the face of the LORD is against those who do
evil.

—1 Peter 3:12

Acts 23:11 says: *But the following night the Lord stood by him and said, "Be of good cheer, Paul; for as you have testified for Me in Jerusalem, so you must also bear witness at Rome."*

There are three important things to notice in that verse.

First, God stands by us in times of unanswered prayer. It says, *The Lord stood by him.* The Lord Jesus Christ came down to stand beside him in that prison cell. When we face unanswered prayer and when our hopes and dreams are dashed, the Lord Himself comes down to stand with us.

Second, He commands us to be of good cheer in the face of unanswered prayer. Don't be discouraged. Don't give in to disappointment. Don't despair. Change your mental attitude and start rejoicing. Count it all joy. Trust God anyway and rejoice. This disappointment is His appointment. Our "Plan B's" are often God's "Plan A's."

Third, God knows exactly what He is doing in times of unanswered prayer. *As you have testified for Me in Jerusalem, so you must also bear witness at Rome.* The Lord hasn't really failed to answer our prayers. He has simply—substituted.

We reach a new plateau in our Christian faith and discover a new aspect of God's omnipotence on our behalf when we learn to trust Him with unanswered prayer and to thank Him for what His love denies. For in such times He stands with us. He tells us to be of good cheer. And He reminds us that He is still in control and that He knows exactly what He is doing.

—Robert J. Morgan

And Satan trembles when he see the weakest saint upon his knees.

—William Cowper

*Continue to pray as you are directed by
the Holy Spirit.*
—Jude 1:20 NLT

But maybe prayer is a road to rise, a mountain path leading toward the skies to assist the spirit who truly tries. . . . It isn't a pack-horse to carry your load, it isn't a wagon, it's only a road. And perhaps the reward of the spirit who tries is not the goal, but the exercise!

—Edmund Vance Cooke

He prayeth best who loveth best All things, both great and small.

—Samuel Taylor Coleridge

Listen to my cry for help, my King and my God, for to you I pray.
—Psalm 5:2 NIV

Prayer takes place in the heart, not in the head.

—Carlo Carretto

Each exclamation is a trigger to prayer. I find myself praying for you with a glad heart.
—Philippians 1:4 THE MESSAGE

God answers sharp and sudden on some prayers, And thrusts the thing we have prayed for in our face, A gauntlet with a gift in it.

—**Elizabeth Barrett Browning**

April

Yet then from all my grief, O Lord, Thy mercy set me free, Whilst in the confidence of pray'r, My soul took hold on thee.

—Joseph Addison

Therefore we also pray always for you that our God would count you worthy of this calling, and fulfill all the good pleasure of His goodness and the work of faith with power.
—2 Thessalonians 1:11

Life-giving heavenly bread, feed me, sanctify me, reign in me, transform me to yourself, live in me, and let me live in you . . . listen to you as my master, obey you as my king, imitate you as my model, follow you as my shepherd, love you as my father, see you as my physician who will heal all the maladies of my soul. Be, indeed my way, truth and life. Sustain me, O heavenly manna, through the desert of this world till I shall behold you unveiled in your glory.

—Elizabeth Seton

I have lived to thank God that all my prayers have not been answered.

—Jean Ingelow

Hear my prayer, O LORD! And let my
cry for help come to You.
— Psalm 102:1 NASB

I pray without ceasing now. My personal prayer is: Make me an instrument which only truth can speak.

—Peace Pilgrim

April

They never sought in vain that sought the Lord aright!

—Robert Burns

If the only prayer you said in your whole life was,
'thank you,' that would suffice.

—**Meister Eckhart**

The LORD is far from the wicked, But He
hears the prayer of the righteous.
—**Proverbs 15:29**

April

It is in vain to expect our prayers to be heard,
if we do not strive as well as pray.

—Aesop

My temple will be called a house
of prayer for all nations.
—Isaiah 56:7 NLT

It may seem a little old-fashioned, always to begin one's work with prayer, but I never undertake a hymn without first asking the good Lord to be my inspiration.

—Fanny Crosby

THE PRAYER OF ST. FRANCIS

Lord, make me a channel of thy peace,

that where there is hatred, I may bring love;

that where there is wrong, I may bring the spirit
of forgiveness;

that where there is discord, I may bring harmony;

that where there is error, I may bring truth;

that where there is doubt, I may bring faith;

that where there is despair, I may bring hope;

that where there are shadows, I may bring light;

that where there is sadness, I may bring joy.

Lord, grant that I may seek rather to comfort than
to be comforted;

to understand, than to be understood;

to love, than to be loved.

For it is by self-forgetting that one finds.

It is by forgiving that one is forgiven.

It is by dying that one awakens to Eternal Life.

—St. Francis

*Our prayer and God's mercy are like two buckets
in a well; while the one ascends the other descends.*

—Mark Hopkins

*Then you will call upon Me and go and pray
to Me, and I will listen to you.*
—Jeremiah 29:12

Prayer begins where human capacity ends.

—Marian Anderson

*My life is one long daily, hourly record of answered prayer.
For physical health . . . for everything that goes to make
up life and my poor service, I can testify with a full and often
wonder-stricken awe that I believe God answers prayer.*

—William of St. Thierry

*I prayed to the LORD my God . . . and said,
"O Lord, great and awesome God, who
keeps His covenant and mercy with those
who love Him, and with those who keep His
commandments.*
—Daniel 9:4

Do not pray for easy lives. Pray to be stronger men. Do not pray for tasks equal to your powers. Pray for powers equal to your tasks.

—Phillips Brooks

I call on you, O God, for you will answer me; give ear to me and hear my prayer.
—Psalm 17:6 NIV

Find me the men on earth who care/ Enough for faith or creed today/
To seek a barren wilderness/ For simple liberty to pray.

—Helen Hunt Jackson

I pray hard, work hard and leave the rest to God.

—Florence Griffith Joyner

I will pray with the spirit, and I will also pray with the understanding. I will sing with the spirit, and I will also sing with the understanding.
—1 Corinthians 14:15

I can give no other testimony. I am sitting alone here on a log among a company of natives. My children, whose very lives are a testimony that God answers prayer, are working round me. Natives are crowding past on the bush road to attend palavers [gatherings], and I am at perfect peace, far from my own countrymen and conditions, because I know God answers prayer. Food is scarce just now . . . . We have not more than will be our breakfast today, but I know we shall be fed, for God answers prayer.

—Mary Slessor, *missionary to Africa*

If thou shouldst never see my face again,
Pray for my soul. More things are wrought by prayer
Than this world dreams of.

—Alfred, Lord Tennyson

Listen to my prayer, O God, do
not ignore my plea.
—Psalm 55:1 NIV

Nothing brings such leanness into a man's soul as lack of prayer. It is well said that neglected prayer is the birthplace of all evil. All good is born in prayer, and all good springs from it. But if one neglects his closet, then all evil comes of it. No man can progress in grace if he forsakes prayer.

—Charles Haddon Spurgeon

The purpose of all prayer is to find God's will and to make that will our prayer.

—Catherine Marshall

Blessed be God, Who has not turned away my prayer, Nor His mercy from me!
—Psalm 66:20

What we need is to see that God's presence is a certain fact always, and that every act of our soul is done right before Him, and that a word spoken in prayer is really spoken to Him, as if our eyes could see Him and our hands could touch Him.

—Billy Graham

April

The shortest distance between a problem and a
solution is the distance between your knees and the floor.

—Charles Stanley

Prayer is the slender nerve that moves the muscle of omnipotence.

—Martin Tupper

*Please help us by praying for us. Then many
people will give thanks for the blessings we
receive in answer to all these prayers.*
—2 Corinthians 1:11 CEV

Dearest Lord, teach me to be generous,
teach me to serve you as I should,
to give and not to count the cost,
to fight and not to heed the wounds,
to toil and not to seek for rest,
to labour and ask not for reward,
save that of knowing that I do your
most holy will.

—St. Ignatius Loyola

*Spread out your petition before God, and then say,
'Thy will be done.' The sweetest lesson I have learned in
God's school is to let the Lord choose for me.*

—Dwight L. Moody

*When my soul fainted within me, I
remembered the LORD; And my prayer went
up to You, Into Your holy temple.*
—Jonah 2:7 KJV

Heaven is too busy to listen to half-hearted prayers or to respond to pop-calls. Our whole being must be in our praying.

—E. M. Bounds

When you pray for anyone you tend to modify your personal attitude toward him.

—**Norman Vincent Peale**

But I say to you, love your enemies, bless those who curse you, do good to those who hate you, and pray for those who spitefully use you and persecute you, that you may be sons of your Father in heaven; for He makes His sun rise on the evil and on the good, and sends rain on the just and on the unjust.

—**Matthew 5:44-45**

The truths that I know best I have learned on my knees.
I never know a thing well, till it is burned into my heart by prayer.

—John Bunyan

*How glad I am that God has taught
me to pray as I run and run as I pray.*

—**John G. Lake**

*But you, when you pray, go into your
room, and when you have shut your door,
pray to your Father who is in the secret
place; and your Father who sees in secret
will reward you openly.*
—**Matthew 6:6**

God delights in our temptations and yet hates them. He delights in them when they drive us to prayer; He hates them when they drive us to despair.

—Martin Luther

The end of all things is near. Therefore be clear minded and self-controlled so that you can pray.
—1 Peter 4:7 NIV

THE FIVE-FINGER PRAYER

Someone sent me this simple way to remember to pray for myself and others—the five-finger prayer.

1. When you clasp your hands in prayer, your thumb is closest to you. Begin your prayer by remembering those closest to you—your children, parents, friends, and other loved ones.

2. The pointing finger is next. Pray for those who point the way: teachers, ministers, and mentors.

3. The tallest finger reminds us to pray for our leaders in government, business, schools, and churches.

4. The ring finger is actually our weakest finger. Pray for those who are sick or in trouble. Ask God to show them that they are weak but He is strong.

5. The smallest finger reminds us that we are to put others before our selves, even in prayer. By the time we have prayed for the needs of the four other groups of people, our own needs will probably seem much less important. The little finger reminds us to pray for ourselves—and to hold to the Bible's promise that "the least shall be the greatest among you."

—Barbara Johnson, *Daily Splashes of Joy*

01 May

*God hears our needs and answers our prayers in the manner
that will help us, serve His will, and often surprise us.*

—Max Lucado

*A revival can be expected when Christians
have the spirit of prayer for revival.*

—Charles Finney

*Watch therefore, and pray always that you
may be counted worthy to escape all these
things that will come to pass, and to stand
before the Son of Man.*
—Luke 21:36

We realize that we are energized by the Holy Spirit for prayer, we know what it is to pray in the atmosphere and the presence of the Holy Spirit; but we do not so often realize that the Holy Spirit himself prays in us with prayers that we cannot utter.

—Oswald Chambers

*There are many people who . . . speak to God in prayer, but
hardly ever listen to Him, or else listen to Him only vaguely.*

—Paul Tournier

*And I will pray the Father, and He will give
you another Helper, that He may abide with
you forever.*
—John 14:16

To believe that God can reach us and bless us in the ordinary junctures of daily life is the stuff of prayer. You see, the only place God can bless us is right where we are, because that is the only place we are!

—Richard J. Foster

Prayer is the gymnasium of the soul.

—Samuel M. Zwemer

When you pray, don't talk on and on as people do who don't know God. They think God likes to hear long prayers.
—Matthew 6:7 CEV

The essence of prayer does not consist in asking God for something but in opening our hearts to God, in speaking with Him, and living with Him in perpetual communion. Prayer is continual abandonment to God. Prayer does not mean asking God for all kinds of things we want; it is rather the desire for God Himself, the only Giver of Life. Prayer is not asking, but union with God. Prayer is not a painful effort to gain from God help in the varying needs of our lives. Prayer is the desire to possess God Himself, the Source of all life. The true spirit of prayer does not consist in asking for blessings, but in receiving Him who is the giver of all blessings, and in living a life of fellowship with Him.

—Sadhu Sundar Singh

*I don't often spend more than half an hour in prayer at one time,
but I never go more than half an hour without praying.*

—Smith Wigglesworth

*Whatever you ask for in prayer with faith,
you will receive.*
—Matthew 21:22 NRSV

You can do more than pray after you have prayed, but you cannot do more than pray until you have prayed.

—A. J. Gordon

He who kneels the most, stands best.

—D. L. Moody

So I tell you, whatever you ask for in prayer, believe that you have received it, and it will be yours.
—Mark 11:24 NRSV

Prayer is asking for the rain and faith is carrying the umbrella.

—Unknown

But I have prayed for you, that your faith should not fail; and when you have returned to Me, strengthen your brethren.
—Luke 22:32

If you have a burden on your back, remember prayer,
for you shall carry it well if you can pray.

—**Charles Haddon Spurgeon**

If we are serious about being spiritual revolutionaries, we must determine to learn how to pray! There are many excellent books on the subject, but there is no substitute for getting on our knees and starting to pray.

—George Verwer

Yea, many people and strong nations shall come to seek the LORD of hosts in Jerusalem, and to pray before the LORD.
—Zechariah 8:22 KJV

THE BEAUTIFUL GARDEN OF PRAYER

There's a garden where Jesus is waiting,
There's a place that is wondrously fair,
For it glows with the light of His presence.
'Tis the beautiful garden of prayer.

There's a garden where Jesus is waiting,
And I go with my burden and care,
Just to learn from His lips words of comfort
In the beautiful garden of prayer.

There's a garden where Jesus is waiting,
And He bids you to come, meet Him there;
Just to bow and receive a new blessing
In the beautiful garden of prayer.

Oh, the beautiful garden, the garden of prayer!
Oh, the beautiful garden of prayer!
There my Savior awaits, and He opens the gates
To the beautiful garden of prayer.

—Eleanor Allen Schroll

The one who kneels to the Lord can stand up to anything.

—Unknown

And when he had sent the multitudes away, he went up into a mountain apart to pray: and when the evening was come, he was there alone.
—Matthew 14:23 KJV

God doesn't always say "Yes" to all our requests, but He listens with unusual attentiveness when two or three gather in united prayer—and He responds in His own way and time with power and wisdom.

—Robert J. Morgan

No one is a firmer believer in the power of prayer than the devil; not that he practices it, but he suffers from it.

—Guy H. King

To be prayerless is to be without God, without Christ, without grace, without hope, and without heaven.

—**J. C. Ryle**

But when you are praying, first forgive anyone you are holding a grudge against, so that your Father in heaven will forgive your sins, too.
—**Mark 11:25** NLT

Lord! thou knowest how busy I must be this day:
if I forget thee, do not thou forget me.

—Sir Jacob Astley

Bless those who curse you, and pray for those
who spitefully use you.
—Luke 6:28

When a man is at his wits' end it is not a cowardly thing to pray,
it is the only way he can get in touch with reality.

—Oswald Chambers

I cannot pray in the name of Jesus to have my own will; the name of Jesus is not a signature of no importance, but the decisive factor. The fact that the name of Jesus comes at the beginning does not make it a prayer in the name of Jesus; but this means to pray in such a manner that I dare name Jesus in it, that is to say, dare to think of Him, think His holy will together with whatever I am praying for.

—Sören Kierkegaard

Prayer is not a substitute for work, thinking, watching, suffering, or giving; prayer is a support for all other efforts.

—George Buttrick

Therefore said he unto them, The harvest truly is great, but the labourers are few: pray ye therefore the Lord of the harvest, that he would send forth labourers into his harvest.
—Luke 10:2 KJV

A family that prays together stays together.

—Unknown

*Treat my prayer as sweet incense rising; my
raised hands are my evening prayers.*
—Psalm 141:2 THE MESSAGE

When a man has done all he can do, still there is a mighty, mysterious agency over which he needs influence to secure success. The one way he can reach it is by prayer.

—Russell H. Conwell

Most men pray for power, the strength to do things.
Few people pray for love, the quality to be someone.

—**Robert D. Foster**

Pray. It isn't a sign of weakness; it is your strength.

—Orville Kelly

So I pray that God, who gives you hope,
will keep you happy and full of peace as you
believe in him. May you overflow with hope
through the power of the Holy Spirit.
—Romans 15:13 NLT

More tears are shed over answered prayers than unanswered ones.

—**Mother Teresa**

*Then Jesus told his disciples a
parable to show them that they
should always pray and not give up.*
— **Luke 18:1** NIV

It is often said that prayer cannot alter the unchangeable purposes of God; but the great scheme of his providence embraces every prayer that shall be offered, as well as the answer it shall receive. It is objected that prayer cannot increase his knowledge of our wants, nor his readiness to supply them; and that in any case he will do what is for the best. But he deems it best to grant many blessings in answer to prayer, which otherwise he would withhold; "He will be very gracious unto thee at the voice of thy cry; when he shall hear it, he will answer thee."

— *American Tract Society Bible Dictionary, 1859*

Prayer should be short, without giving God Almighty reasons why He should grant this, or that; He knows best what is good for us.

—**John Selden**

If something is important to you, it's important to God.

—Max Lucado

"Why are you sleeping?" he asked. "Get up and pray. Otherwise temptation will overpower you."
— Luke 22:46 NLT

Battering the gates of heaven with the storms of prayer.

—**Alfred, Lord Tennyson**

I pray for them. I do not pray for the world but for those whom You have given Me, for they are Yours.
—John 17:9

Resolve to stand strong in the Lord,
even when your prayers have been answered.

—**Stormie Omartian**

Prayer is reaching out to touch Someone—
namely your creator. In the process He touches you.

—Barbara Johnson

Continue in prayer, and watch in
the same with thanksgiving.
—Colossians 4:2 KJV

The best way to get what you pray for is to pray for things for other people. To get things for ourselves, well, that is why God invented work.

—Otto Biel

O Lord, make me more useful for Your work,
More able to perform in Your behalf,
While acting as Your agent on this earth.
I know You will provide the means I need,
To carry out the jobs You give to me.
Please help me to perform the smallest tasks,
Like they were most important in Your eyes.
And then, if I am faithful with the small,
Please give me even greater work to do.
In Jesus' holy name I pray, Amen.

—Rev. Bill McGinnis

Prayer does not equip us for the greater work . . .
prayer is the greater work.

—Oswald Chambers

Pray without ceasing.
—1 Thessalonians 5:17

Prayer is more like listening than anything else—being quiet in God's presence, waiting on God until we know what to do.

—David Roper

Pray all the time, and make it a habit to listen
with all your heart for his voice.

—Luci Swindoll

First of all, then, I urge that supplications,
prayers, intercessions, and thanksgivings
be made for all men, for kings and all
who are in high positions, that we may
lead a quiet and peaceable life, godly and
respectful in every way
—1 Timothy 2:1-2 NRSV

We must not sit still and look for miracles; up and doing,
and the Lord will be with thee. Prayer and pains,
through faith in Christ Jesus, will do anything.

—Sir John Elliott

Repent of this wickedness and pr
to the Lord. Perhaps he will forgi
you for having such a thought i
your heart.
—Acts 8:22 NIV

Prayer lays hold of God's plan and becomes the link between His will and its accomplishment on earth. Amazing things happen, and we are given the privilege of being the channels of the Holy Spirit's prayer.

—Elisabeth Elliot

Prayer is simply a two-way conversation between you and God.

—Billy Graham

But as for me, my prayer is unto thee, O LORD, in an acceptable time: O God, in the multitude of thy mercy hear me, in the truth of thy salvation.
—Psalm 69:13 KJV

GOD HEARS OUR PRAYERS

When [a friend] told Jesus of the illness [of Lazarus] he said, "Lord the one you love is sick." He doesn't base his appeal on the imperfect love of the one in need, but on the perfect love of the Savior. He doesn't say, "The one *who loves you* is sick." He says "The one you love is sick." The power of the prayer, in other words, does not depend on the one who makes the prayer, but on the one who hears the prayer.

We can and must repeat the phrase in manifold ways. "The one you love is tired, sad, hungry, lonely, fearful, depressed." The words of the prayer vary, but the response never changes. The Savior hears the prayer. He silences heaven, so He won't miss a word. He hears the prayer.

—Max Lucado, *The Great House of God.*

Never let your head hang down. Never give up and sit down and grieve. Find another way. And don't pray when it rains if you don't pray when the sun shines.

—Leroy "Satchel" Paige

Jesus commands us to 'watch and pray.' If we are able to be persons of faith, then we will be persons of prayer. If we are to be persons of hope and healing in the world, then we will be persons for whom living is praying, and praying is living. In short, we have no choice but to pray.

—Conrad Hoover

Watch and pray, lest you enter into temptation. The spirit indeed is willing, but the flesh is weak.
—Matthew 26:41

Faith in a prayer-hearing God will make a prayer-loving Christian.

—Andrew Murray

*I want men everywhere to lift up holy hands
in prayer, without anger or disputing.*
—1 Timothy 2:8 NIV

The joy and pleasure of speaking with the Lord is far superior to anything life on this earth affords. Through prayer I become centered and serene. When it's quiet and still, I sense the Lord comes near as I enter his presence.

—Luci Swindoll

We must alter our lives in order to alter our hearts,
for it is impossible to live one way and pray another.

—William Law

God warms his hands at man's heart when he prays.

—John Masefield

Anyone who is having troubles should pray.
Anyone who is happy should sing praises.
—James 5:13 NCV

THE APOSTLE'S CREED

I believe in God the Father, Almighty,
Maker of heaven and earth:
And in Jesus Christ, his only begotten
Son, our Lord:
Who was conceived by the Holy
Ghost, born of the Virgin Mary:
Suffered under Pontius Pilate; was
crucified, dead and buried: He
descended into hell:
The third day he rose again from the
dead:
He ascended into heaven, and sits
at the right hand of God the Father
Almighty:
From thence he shall come to judge
the quick and the dead:
I believe in the Holy Ghost:
I believe in the holy catholic church:
the communion of saints:
The forgiveness of sins:
The resurrection of the body:
And the life everlasting. Amen.

The more praying there is in the world, the better the world will be, the mightier the forces against evil everywhere.

—E. M. Bounds

And the prayer of faith will save the sick, and the Lord will raise him up.
—James 5:15

Prayer teaches trust in God through waiting upon *His* timing.

—**Becky Tirabassi**

And the prayer of faith will
save the sick, and the Lord will
raise him up.
—**James 5:15**

Prayer is not merely an occasional impulse to which we respond when we are in trouble: prayer is a life attitude.

—**Walter A. Mueller**

Work as if you were to live a hundred years.
Pray as if you were to die tomorrow.

— **Benjamin Franklin**

Prayer is the place where burdens are shifted.

—Barbara Johnson

Hear my voice, O God, in my meditation.
—Psalm 64:1

Those who know God the best are the richest and most powerful in prayer. Little acquaintance with God, and strangeness and coldness to Him, make prayer a rare and feeble thing.

— **E. M. Bounds**

Let my prayer come before thee; incline thine ear to my cry.
—**Psalm 88:2** NASV

When I began to pray with all my heart, everything around me seemed delightful and marvelous. The trees, the grass, the birds, the earth, the air, the light seemed to be telling me that they existed for man's sake, that they witnessed to the love of God for man, that all things prayed to God and sang his praise. This it was that I came to understand what the *Philokalia* calls 'the knowledge of the speech of all creatures.'

—Unknown

This is our Lord's will . . . that our prayer and our trust be alike, large. For if we do not trust as much as we pray, we fail in full worship to our Lord in our prayer; and also we hinder and hurt ourselves.

—Julian of Norwich

God does not stand afar off as I struggle to speak.
He cares enough to listen with more than casual attention.
He translates my scrubby words and hears what is truly inside.
He hears my sighs and uncertain gropings as fine prose.

—Timothy Jones

But we will give ourselves continually to
prayer, and to the ministry of the word.
—Acts 6:4 KJV

Rich is the person who has a praying friend.

—Janice Hughes

Pray first that the Lord's message will spread rapidly and be honored wherever it goes, just as when it came to you.
—2 Thessalonians 3:1

Is prayer your steering wheel or your spare tire?

—Corrie ten Boom

Prayer is talking with God and telling Him you love Him, conversing with God about all the things that are important in life, both large and small, and being assured that He is listening.

—**C. Neil Strait**

God does nothing but in answer to prayer.

—John Wesley

Pray for us; for we are confident that we have a good conscience, in all things desiring to live honorably.
—Hebrews 13:18

THE 23RD PSALM

The Lord is my shepherd; I shall not want.
He maketh me to lie down in green pastures:
he leadeth me beside the still waters.
He restoreth my soul: he leadeth me in the
paths of righteousness for his name's sake.
Yea, though I walk through the valley of
the shadow of death, I will fear no evil: for
thou art with me; thy rod and thy staff they
comfort me.
Thou preparest a table before me in the
presence of mine enemies: thou anointest my
head with oil; my cup runneth over.
Surely goodness and mercy shall follow me
all the days of my life: and I will dwell in the
house of the Lord for ever.

—Psalm 23:1–6 KJV

Prayer opens the heart to God, and it is the means by which the soul, though empty, is filled by God.

—John Bunyan

Lord, every morning you hear my voice.
Every morning, I tell you what I need, and I
wait for your answer.
—Psalm 5:3 NCV

When a Christian shuns fellowship with other Christians, the devil smiles. When he stops studying the Bible, the devil laughs. When he stops praying, the devil shouts for joy.

—Corrie ten Boom

All this trying leads up to the vital moment at which you turn to God and say, "You must do this. I can't."

—**C. S. Lewis**

Also, the Spirit helps us with our weakness. We do not know how to pray as we should. But the Spirit himself speaks to God for us, even begs God for us with deep feelings that words cannot explain.
—**Romans 8:28** NCV

*Let this be thy whole endeavor, this thy prayer, this
thy desire,—that thou mayest be stripped of all selfishness,
and with entire simplicity follow Jesus only.*

—Thomas à Kempis

*Give ear, O LORD, to my prayer;And attend
to the voice of my supplications.*
—Psalm 86:6

We must move from asking God to take care of the things that are breaking our hearts, to praying about the things that are breaking His heart.

—Margaret Gibb

Prayer has comforted us in sorrow and
will help strengthen us for the journey ahead.

—George W. Bush

Peace I leave with you; my
peace I give you. I do not give to
you as the world gives. Do not
let your hearts be troubled and
do not be afraid.
—John 14:27

GOD IN THE DETAILS

Often Christians ask, "Isn't it selfish to pray about the petty details of everyday living?"

No, not if we take Jesus' word on this. The total stream of our lives is made of the sum of just such details. When we ask for God's help only in the major decisions, we are admitting Him into a very small part of our lives.

Watch Jesus stride through the Gospels. He concerned Himself with peoples' health problems; with securing the money for Peter's tax; with the contents of one little boy's lunch box, so the hungry crowds could be fed; with a woman who lost one coin out of her wedding necklace; with one lost sheep.

This is the message of the Bible from the beginning to the end—not only that God cares about the individual, but that no detail of the individual's life is too small for His loving concern.

—Catherine Marshall,
Moments that Matter

Nothing can keep you from being directly connected to God if you want to be.

—Thelma Wells

Don't stop praying even if you've been doing it for a long time and it seems as if God must not be listening.

—Stormie Omartian

If any of you lacks wisdom, let him ask of God, who gives to all liberally and without reproach, and it will be given to him.

—James 1:5

Pray, and let God worry.

—**Martin Luther**

I will never leave you or forsake you.
—**Hebrews 13:5**

*I have had prayers answered — most strangely sometimes —
but I think our heavenly Father's loving kindness has
been even more evident in what He has refused me.*

—Lewis Carroll

Prayer is an ordinance of God, that must continue with a soul so long as it is on this side glory.

—John Bunyan

But his delight is in the law of the LORD,
And in His law he meditates day and night.
—Psalm 1:2

God's hearing of our prayers doth not depend upon sanctification, but upon Christ's intercession; not upon what we are in ourselves, but what we are in the Lord Jesus; both our persons and our prayers are acceptable in the beloved.

—**Thomas Brooks**

The practice of the Jesus prayer is simple. Stand before the Lord with the attention in the heart, and call to him: 'Lord Jesus Christ, Son of God, have mercy on me!' The essential part of this is not in the words, but in faith, contrition, and self-surrender to the Lord. With these feelings one can stand before the Lord even without any words, and it will still be prayer.

—Theophan the Recluse

*A simple grateful thought turned heavenwards
is the most perfect prayer.*

—Gotthold Lessing

*Until now you have asked nothing in My
name. Ask, and you will receive, that your
joy may be full.*
—John 16:24

Keep praying, but be thankful that God's answers are wiser than your prayers.

—**William Culbertson**

Prayer is as natural an expression of faith as breathing is of life.

—Jonathan Edwards

If you ask anything in My name, I will do it.
—John 14:14

Prayer is our path to the adventure of building a relationship with our Savior.

Christa Kinde

I meditate within my heart, And my spirit makes diligent search.
—Psalm 77:6

Prayer has mighty power to move mountains because the Holy Spirit is ready both to encourage our praying and to remove the mountains hindering us. Prayer has the power to change mountains into highways.

—**Wesley L. Duewel**

Prayer is not so much an act as it is an attitude —
an attitude of dependency, dependency upon God.

—Arthur W. Pink

Again I say to you that if two of you
agree on earth concerning anything
that they ask, it will be done for them
by My Father in heaven.
—Matthew 18:19

PRAYER IS THE SOUL'S SINCERE DESIRE

Prayer is the soul's sincere desire,
Unuttered or expressed;
The motion of a hidden fire
That trembles in the breast.

Prayer is the burden of a sigh,
The falling of a tear
The upward glancing of an eye,
When none but God is near.

Prayer is the Christian's vital breath,
The Christian's native air,
His watchword at the gates of death;
He enters Heav'n with prayer.

Prayer is the contrite sinner's voice,
Returning from his ways,
While angels in their songs rejoice
And cry, "Behold, he prays!"

No prayer is made by man alone
The Holy Spirit pleads,
And Jesus, on th'eternal throne,
For sinners intercedes.

O Thou by Whom we come to God,
The Life, the Truth, the Way,
The path of prayer Thyself hast trod:
Lord, teach us how to pray.

—James Montgomery

Ask God's blessing on your work, but don't ask him to do it for you.

—Dame Flora Robson

The righteous cry out, and the LORD hears,
And delivers them out of all their troubles.
—Psalm 34:17

I've decided to change the way I pray. I used to pray with a whole long list of things I wanted God to do; now I pray for wisdom, and I pray to be more like Christ.

—**Sheila Walsh**

There are some favors the Almighty does not grant either the first, or the second, or the third time you ask Him, because He wishes you to pray for a long time and often. He wills this delay to keep you in a state of humility and self-contempt and make you realize the value of His graces.

—**John Eudes**

Whatsoever we beg of God, let us also work for it.

—Jeremy Taylor

Those that wait upon the LORD shall renew their strength.
—Isaiah 40:31

When we fail to pray, we aren't cheating God, we're cheating ourselves.

—Thelma Wells

Create in me a clean heart, O God, And
renew a steadfast spirit within me.
—Psalm 51:10

Those blessings are sweetest that are won with prayers and worn with thanks.

—Thomas Goodwin

In our praying, we should speak to God about Himself that is praise; or about His gifts that is thanksgiving; or about other people that is intercession; or about our sins that is confession and penitence; or about our needs that is petition. Prayer has five fingers, like a hand, and each in turn must be pointed to God, that our prayer may be full and complete.

—F. W. Kates

The quiet hour of prayer is one of the most favorable opportunities He has in which to speak to us seriously. In quietude and solitude before the face of God, our souls can hear better than at any other time.

—**O. Hallesby**

Come to Me, all you who labor and are heavy laden, and I will give you rest.
—**Matthew 11:28**

August

I have been driven many times to my knees by the overwhelming conviction that I had absolutely no other place to go.

—Abraham Lincoln

But do not forget to do good and to share, for with such sacrifices God is well pleased.
—Hebrews 14:16

Our prayers may be awkward. Our attempts may be feeble.
But since the power of prayer is in the one who hears it and
not in the one who says it, our prayers do make a difference.

—**Max Lucado**

'The one concern of the devil is to keep the saints from prayer. He fears nothing from prayerless studies, prayerless work, prayerless religion. He laughs at our toil, mocks at our wisdom, but trembles when we pray.

—Samuel Chadwick

My kindness is all you need. My power is strongest when you are weak.
—2 Corinthians 12:9 CEV

Whenever I happen to be prevented by the press of duties from observing my hour of prayer, the entire day is bad for me.

—Martin Luther

August

Courage is fear that has said its prayers.

—Dorothy Bernard

Please let Your ear be attentive and Your eyes open, that You may hear the prayer of Your servant which I pray before You now, day and night.

—Nehemiah 1:6

AN EVENING PRAYER

If I have wounded any soul today,
If I have caused one foot to go astray,
If I have walked in my own willful way,
Dear Lord, forgive!

If I have uttered idle words or vain,
If I have turned aside from want or pain,
Lest I myself shall suffer through the strain,
Dear Lord, forgive!

If I have been perverse or hard, or cold,
If I have longed for shelter in Thy fold,
When Thou hast given me some fort to hold,
Dear Lord, forgive!

Forgive the sins I have confessed to Thee;
Forgive the secret sins I do not see;
O guide me, love me and my keeper be,
Dear Lord, Amen.

—C. Maude Battersby

The discussion of prayer is so great that it requires the
Father to reveal it, His firstborn Word to teach it, and the
Spirit to enable us to think and speak rightly of so great a subject.

—**Origen**

Prayer involves transformed passions. In prayer, real prayer, we begin to think God's thoughts after Him: to desire the things He desires, to love the things He loves, to will the things He wills.

—**Richard J. Foster**

And if we know that He hears us, whatever we ask, we know that we have the petitions that we have asked of Him.
—**1 John 5:15**

August

In quiet conversations with our Lord, we hear in our
longing hearts of His expansive love, which helps
us to move from our inner conflict to His peaceful resolution.

—Patsy Clairmont

He went in therefore, shut the door behind
the two of them, and prayed to the LORD.
—2 Kings 4:33

We forget that God sometimes has to say No. We pray to Him as our heavenly Father, and like wise human fathers, He often says, No, not from whim or caprice, but from wisdom and from love, and knowing what is best for us.

—**Peter Marshall**

Whether we think of, or speak to, God, whether we act or suffer for Him, all is prayer, when we have no other object than His love, and the desire of pleasing Him.

—John Wesley

Prayer cannot be measured in terms of 'usefulness.'
It can only be understood as a complete surrender
without wanting 'to get something out of it.'

—Peter G. Van Breemen

GOD, you're my last chance of the day. I
spend the night on my knees before you.
—Psalm 88:1 THE MESSAGE

What a Friend We Have in Jesus

What a friend we have in Jesus,
All our sins and griefs to bear;
What a privilege to carry
Ev'rything to God in prayer!

O what peace we often forfeit,
O what needless pain we bear.
Just because we do not carry
Ev'rything to God in prayer.

Have we trials and temptations?
Is there trouble anywhere?
We should never be discouraged;
Take it to the Lord in prayer.

Can we find a friend so faithful,
Who will all our sorrows share?
Jesus knows our ev'ry weakness;
Take it to the Lord in prayer.

Are we weak and heavy-laden,
Cumbered with a load of care?
Precious Saviour, still our refuge;
Take it to the Lord in prayer.

Do thy friends despise, forsake thee?
Take it to the Lord in prayer;
In His arms He'll take and shield thee,
Thou wilt find a solace there. Amen.

—Joseph Scriven

Our responsibility is to keep knocking at God's door . . .
to keep believing God will answer our prayers. . . .
Patiently but expectantly wait on the Lord.

—Thelma Wells

My prayer is pure.
—Job 16:17

When you are in the dark, listen, and God
will give you a very precious message.

—Oswald Chambers

_____
_____
_____
_____
_____
_____
_____
_____
_____
_____
_____
_____
_____
_____
_____
_____
_____
_____
_____

Thus says the LORD, the God of
David your father: "I have heard
your prayer, I have seen your tears;
surely I will heal you."
—2 Kings 20:5

Nothing tends more to cement the hearts of Christians than praying together. Never do they love one another so well as when they witness the outpouring of each other's hearts in prayer.

—Charles Finney

Through prayer, God greatly multiplies our efforts. What we can do on our own is limited, but what God can do is endless.
—**John Maxwell**

Promises are the golden fruit to be picked by the hands of prayer.

—**E. M. Bounds**

*Be merciful, O Lord, for I am calling
on you constantly.*
—**Psalm 86:3** NLT

19   August

The best and sweetest flowers of Paradise God gives
to His people when they are upon their knees.
Prayer is the gate of heaven, a key to let us in to Paradise.
—Thomas Brooks

There come times when I have nothing more to tell God. If I were to continue to pray in words, I would have to repeat what I have already said. At such times it is wonderful to say to God, "May I be in Thy presence, Lord? I have nothing more to say to Thee, but I do love to be in Thy presence."

—O. Hallesby

Our God takes care of everyone who truly worships him, but that he gets very angry and punishes anyone who refuses to obey. We went without food and asked God himself to protect us, and he answered our prayers.
—Ezra 8:23 CEV

August

Always respond to every impulse to pray. The impulse to pray may come when you are reading or when you are battling with a text. I would make an absolute law of this — always obey such an impulse.

—**Martyn Lloyd-Jones**

To clasp hands in prayer is the beginning of an uprising against the disorder in the world.

—**Karl Barth**

Trust in Him at all times, you people;
Pour out your heart before Him; God is
a refuge for us.
—**Psalm 62:8**

He who prays as he ought will endeavour to live as he prays.

—**John Owen**

Perhaps one reason God delays His answers to our prayers is because He knows we need to be with Him far more than we need the things we ask of Him.

—Ben Patterson

Hear me when I call, O God of my righteousness!
You have relieved me in my distress;
Have mercy on me, and hear my prayer.
—Psalm 4:1

I have been benefited by praying for others; for by making an errand to God for them I have gotten something for myself.

—S. Rutherford

Yet give attention to your servant's prayer and his plea for mercy, O LORD my God. Hear the cry and the prayer that your servant is praying in your presence.
—2 Chronicles 6:19 NIV

Fear not because your prayer is stammering, your words feeble, and your language poor. Jesus can understand you. Just as a mother understands the first lispings of her infant, so does the blessed Savior understand sinners. He can read a sigh, and see a meaning in a groan.

—J. C. Ryle

THE PRAYER OF JABEZ

And Jabez called on the God of Israel saying,
"Oh, that You would bless me indeed,
and enlarge my territory,
that Your hand would be with me,
and that You would keep me from evil,
that I may not cause pain!"
So God granted him what he requested.

—1 Chronicles 4:10

The man who is willing to pray, but realizes he does not know how to do it, can hardly do better than to start with thanks.

—Elton Trueblood

You are forgiving and good, O Lord, abounding in love to all who call to you.
—Psalm 86:5

August

When you want to communicate with someone who wants to communicate with you and who has all the answers to your questions, call Him up.

—**Thelma Wells**

Choose gentleness . . . Nothing is won by force. I choose to be gentle. If I raise my voice may it be only in praise. If I clench my fist, may it be only in prayer. If I make a demand, may it be only of myself.

—Max Lucado

I have sinned greatly in what I have done; but now, I pray, O LORD, take away the iniquity of Your servant, for I have done very foolishly.
—2 Samuel 24:10

August

The men who have guided the destiny of the United States have found the strength for their tasks by going to their knees. This private unity of public men and their God is an enduring source of reassurance for the people of America.

—Lyndon B. Johnson

Dear boy, I should like you to preach, but it is best that you pray. Many a preacher has proved a castaway, but never one person who had truly learned to pray.

—Charles Haddon Spurgeon

It is written, "My house is a house of prayer."
—Luke 19:46

Prayer is never an acceptable substitute for obedience. The sovereign Lord accepts no offering from His creatures that is not accompanied by obedience.

—A. W. Tozer

In the day of my trouble I will call upon You, For You will answer me.
—Psalm 86:7

Ceaseless interior prayer is a continual yearning of the human spirit towards God. To succeed in this consoling exercise we must pray more often to God to teach us to pray without ceasing. Pray more, and pray more fervently. It is prayer itself which will reveal to you how it can be achieved unceasingly; but it will take some time.

—Unknown

September

God can change our circumstances, but sometimes
He waits for us to show real desire for change as well as our faith in Him.

—Anne Graham Lotz

Go to bed seasonably, and rise early. Redeem your precious time: pick up the fragments of it, that not one moment of it may be lost. Be much in secret prayer. Converse less with man, and more with God.

—George Whitefield

In everything give thanks; for this is the will of God in Christ Jesus for you.
—1 Thessalonians 5:18

September

Prayer should be the key of the day and the lock of the night.

—**George Herbert**

You do not have because you do not ask.
—**James 4:2**

Almighty God, unto whom all hearts are open,
all desires known, and from whom no secrets are hid:
Cleanse the thoughts of our hearts by the inspiration of thy Holy
Spirit, that we may perfectly love thee, and worthily magnify
thy holy Name; through Jesus Christ our Lord. Amen.

—Book of Common Prayer

September

When you pray, ask God to reveal His will for your life and he situation you are facing. Don't just get caught up in praying for material gain. God provides where there is a need. His greatest desire is for you to learn to trust him in prayer.

—Charles Stanley

*Grant that I may not pray alone with the mouth; help me that
I may pray from the depths of my heart.*

—Martin Luther

*The Lord is near to all who call upon Him,
To all who call upon Him in truth.*
—Psalm 145:18

Oh Lord, may I be directed what
to do and what to leave undone;
and then may I humbly trust that
a blessing will be with me in my
various engagements. . . . Enable
me, O Lord, to feel tenderly and
charitably toward all my beloved
fellow mortals . . . Let me walk in all
humility and Godly fear before all
men, and in their sight.

—Elizabeth Fry

Someone once said that prayer is the key to the morning and the bolt to the evening. Another person wrote that a day hemmed in prayer seldom comes unraveled. There are no shortcuts: Spiritual vitality depends on a regular and rigorous habit of daily prayer.

—Robert J. Morgan

But it is good for me to draw near to God; I have put my trust in the Lord GOD, That I may declare all Your works.
—Psalm 73:28

Every Christian needs a half an hour of prayer each day, except when he is busy, then he needs an hour.

—**St. Francis de Sales**

Get down on your knees and thank God you're still on your feet.

—Irish proverb

*Delight yourself also in the Lord, And He
shall give you the desires of your heart.*
—Psalm 37:4

The Christian life is not a constant high. I have my moments of deep discouragement. I have to go to God in prayer with tears in my eyes, and say, "O God, forgive me," or "Help me."

—**Billy Graham**

If you begin to live life looking for the God that is all around you, every moment becomes a prayer.

—Frank Bianco

The Spirit helps us in our weakness. We do not know what we ought to pray for, but the Spirit himself intercedes for us with groans that words cannot express.
—Romans 8:26 NIV

I pray and meditate every single day, every morning. You know, I pray in cabs. I pray in airplanes. I don't really ask for anything. I just pray that Jesus will give me the strength to follow Him. That's all I pray for. And that I will always turn my will and my life over to His care.

—Lawrence Kudlow

Praise the LORD.
Praise God in his sanctuary;
praise him in his mighty heavens.
Praise him for his acts of power;
praise him for his surpassing greatness.
Praise him with the sounding of the trumpet,
praise him with the harp and lyre,
praise him with tambourine and dancing,
praise him with the strings and flute,
praise him with the clash of cymbals,
praise him with resounding cymbals.
Let everything that has breath praise the LORD .
Praise the LORD.

—Psalm 150:1–6, NIV

*"Again I say to you that if two of you
agree on earth concerning anything
that they ask, it will be done for them
by My Father in heaven."*
—Matthew 18:19

September

We need to learn to know Him so well that we feel safe when we have left our difficulties with Him. To know Jesus in that way is a prerequisite of all true prayer.

—**O. Hallesby**

*To pray is nothing more involved than to open the door,
giving Jesus access to our needs and permitting Him
to exercise His own power in dealing with them.*

—O. Hallesby

*For where two or three are gathered
together in My name, I am there in
the midst of them.*
—Matthew 18:20

September

It is possible to move men, through God, by prayer alone.

—James Hudson Taylor

I meditate on You in the night watches.
—Psalm 63:6

*No one who has had a unique experience
with prayer has a right to withhold it from others.*

—Soong Mei-ling

Lord, show me an open door. Lord, open my eyes to the person you want me to evangelize. Lord, give me a soul. Lord, use me in someone's life. Pray for open doors.

—Robert J. Morgan

Everyone prays in their own language, and there is no language that God does not understand.

—Duke Ellington

What other nation is so great as to have their gods near them the way the LORD our God is near us whenever we pray to him?
—Deuteronomy 4:7 NIV

SWEET HOUR OF PRAYER

Sweet hour of prayer! sweet hour of prayer!
That calls me from a world of care,
And bids me at my Father's throne
Make all my wants and wishes known.
In seasons of distress and grief,
My soul has often found relief
And oft escaped the tempter's snare
By thy return, sweet hour of prayer!

Sweet hour of prayer! sweet hour of prayer!
The joys I feel, the bliss I share,
Of those whose anxious spirits burn
With strong desires for thy return!
With such I hasten to the place
Where God my Savior shows His face,
And gladly take my station there,
And wait for thee, sweet hour of prayer!

Sweet hour of prayer! sweet hour of prayer!
Thy wings shall my petition bear
To Him whose truth and faithfulness
Engage the waiting soul to bless.
And since He bids me seek His face,
Believe His Word and trust His grace,
I'll cast on Him my every care,
And wait for thee, sweet hour of prayer!

—William Walford

Trouble and perplexity drive me to prayer and prayer drives away perplexity and trouble.

—Philip Melanchthen

Bow down Your ear, O LORD, hear me.
—Psalm 86:1

The value of consistent prayer is not that
He will hear us, but that we will hear Him.

— **William McGill**

We have to pray with our eyes on God, not on the difficulties.

—Oswald Chambers

*Draw near to God and He will
draw near to you.*
—James 4:8

When at night you cannot sleep, talk to the Shepherd and stop counting sheep.

—Unknown

Then he turned his face toward the wall, and prayed to the LORD.
—2 Kings 20:2

Prayer is not merely an occasional impulse to which we respond when we are in trouble: prayer is a life attitude.

—**Walter A. Mueller**

September

If you are worried about someone today, or about yourself . . .
If you are finding your stomach knotting, your head pounding,
and your teeth clenched, remember this: The best remedy for a
knotted stomach or a pounding head is the bent knee.

—Robert J. Morgan

Grant me, oh Lord my God,
a mind to know you,
a heart to seek you,
wisdom to find you,
conduct pleasing to you,
faithful perseverance in
waiting for you
and a hope of finally
embracing you.

—Thomas Aquinas

*I love the LORD, because He has heard my
voice and my supplications. Because He has
inclined His ear to me, therefore I will call
upon Him as long as I live.*
—Psalm 116:1-2

Make it a rule, and pray to God to help you to keep it, never,
if possible, to lie down at night without being able to say:
"I have made one human being at least a little wiser, or
a little happier, or at least a little better this day."

—**Charles Kingsley**

Prayer is when you talk to God; meditation is when you listen to God.

—**Unknown**

I will call upon the LORD, who is worthy to be praised; So shall I be saved from my enemies.
—**Psalm 18:3**

The trouble with our praying is, we just do it as a means of last resort.

—Will Rogers

*I will also meditate on all
Your work, And talk of
Your deeds.*
—Psalm 77:12

When you pray, rather let your heart be without words than your words without heart.

—John Bunyan

Courage is fear that has said its prayers.

—**Karl Barth**

*I believe in prayer. It's the best way we have
to draw strength from heaven.*

—Josephine Baker

*But without faith it is impossible to please
Him, for he who comes to God must believe
that He is, and that He is a rewarder of those
who diligently seek Him.*
—Hebrews 11:6

Prayer is not an indifferent or a small thing. It is not a sweet little privilege. It is a great prerogative, far-reaching in its effects. Failure to pray entails losses far beyond the person who neglects it. Prayer is not a mere episode of the Christian life. Rather the whole life is a preparation for and the result of prayer. In its condition, prayer is the sum of religion. Faith is but a channel of prayer. Faith gives it wings and swiftness. Prayer is the lungs through which holiness breathes. Prayer is not only the language of spiritual life, but makes its very essence and forms its real character.

—E. M. Bounds

Certain thoughts are prayers. There are moments when, whatever be the attitude of the body, the soul is on its knees.

—Victor Hugo

And whatever you ask in My name, that I will do, that the Father may be glorified in the Son.
—John 14:13

God can pick sense out of a confused prayer.

—**Richard Sibbes**

Prayer requires more of the heart than of the tongue.

—Adam Clarke

And whatever we ask we receive from Him,
because we keep His commandments and do
those things that are pleasing in His sight.
—1 John 3:22

God always answers our prayers, but sometimes the answer is no.

—Unknown

God speaks in the silence of the heart.
Listening is the beginning of prayer.

—Mother Teresa

And in that day you will ask Me nothing.
Most assuredly, I say to you, whatever you ask
the Father in My name He will give you.
—John 16:23

Prayer is not monologue, but dialogue; God's voice is its most essential part. Listening to God's voice is the secret of the assurance that He will listen to mine.

—Andrew Murray

Meditate within your heart on your bed, and be still.
—Psalm 4:4

Oh my God, I ask of you for myself
and for those whom I hold dear,
the grace to fulfill perfectly your holy will,
to accept for love of you the joys and
sorrows of this passing life,
so that we may one day be united in
Heaven for all eternity.

— Theresa of Lisieux

A good man is not a perfect man; a good man is an honest man, faithful, and unhesitatingly responsive to the voice of God in his life.

— **John Fischer**

God's heart is the most sensitive and tender of all.
No act goes unnoticed, no matter how insignificant or small.

—Richard J. Foster

Now this is the confidence that we have in Him, that if we ask anything according to His will, He hears us.
—1 John 5:14

Prayer does not cause faith to work, faith causes prayer to work.

—Gloria Copeland

Prayer draws us near to our own souls.

—Herman Melville

You can be sure of this: The LORD has set apart the godly for himself. The LORD will answer when I call to him.
—Psalm 4:3 NLT

Prayer is nothing but the breathing that out before the Lord, that was first breathed into us by the Spirit of the Lord.

—**Thomas Brooks**

*We must move from asking God to take care
of the things that are breaking our hearts, to praying
about the things that are breaking His heart.*

—Margaret Gibb

*Let me understand the teaching of your
precepts; then I will meditate on your
wonders.*
—Psalm 119:27 NIV

There's a blessing in prayer,
in believing prayer,
When our Savior's Name
to the throne we bear;
Then a Father's love will
receive us there;
There is always a blessing, a
blessing in prayer.

—Eliza E. Hewitt

The eyes of the LORD are on the righteous,
And His ears are open to their cry.
—Psalm 34:15

Our prayers should be for blessings in general, for God knows best what is good for us.

—Socrates

Just pray for a tough hide and a tender heart.

—Ruth Bell Graham

God tells us to burden him with whatever burdens us.

—Unknown

Enter into his gates with thanksgiving, and into his courts with praise: be thankful unto him, and bless his name.
—Psalm 100:4 KJV

Who rises from prayer a better man, his prayer is answered.

—George Meredith

When they call on me, I will answer;
I will be with them in trouble. I will
rescue them and honor them.
—Psalm 91:15 NLT

God has editing rights over our prayers. He will . . .
edit them, correct them, bring them in line with His will
and then hand them back to us to be resubmitted.

—Stephen Crotts

The purpose of prayer is not to get answers, things or anything—
not even holiness. Valuable though they are, all
of those are side effects. The purpose of prayer is to
get acquainted with God. Anything else is a bonus.
—Alfred C. McClure

It shall come to pass, That before they call,
I will answer; And while they are still
speaking, I will hear.
—Isaiah 65:24

HE WILL ANSWER EVERY PRAYER

God has given you His promise
That He hears and answers prayer.
He will heed your supplication
If you cast on Him your care.

He will not withhold one blessing,
He will give you what is best.
God will answer by His Spirit,
Every one who makes request.

He can hear the great petition,
And the smallest, over there.
Unto God pray without ceasing,
He will answer every prayer.

Take to God your plans and failures,
Any time and anywhere.
No one ever goes unanswered,
For He answers every prayer.

He will answer every prayer,
He will answer every prayer,
Go to Him in faith believing,
He will answer every prayer.

—Mary Bernstecher

October

We must focus on prayer as the main thrust to accomplish God's will and purpose on earth. The forces against us have never been greater and this is the only way we can release God's power to become victorious.

—John Maxwell

How often has God said no to my earnest prayers that He might answer my deepest longings, give me something more, something better.

—Ruth Bell Graham

Everyone will come to you because you answer prayer.
—Psalm 65:2 CEV

Prayer is reaching out to touch Someone—namely your creator. In the process He touches you.

—Barbara Johnson

Prayer is the language of a man burdened with a sense of need.

—E. M. Bounds

Give us help from trouble.
—Psalm 60:11 KJV

November

God, forgive the poverty and the pettiness of our prayers.
Listen not to our words but to the yearnings of our hearts.
Hear beneath our petitions the crying of our need.

—Peter Marshall

Prayer is exhaling the spirit of man and inhaling the spirit of God.

—Edwin Keith

God knows how often I pray for you. Day and night I bring you and your needs in prayer to God.
—Romans 1:9 NLT

EVENING PRAYER

My Heavenly Father, I thank You,
through Jesus Christ, Your beloved Son,
that You have protected me,
by Your grace.
Forgive, I pray, all my sins and
the evil I have done.
Protect me, by Your grace, tonight.
I put myself in your care, body and soul
and all that I have.
Let Your holy angels be with me,
so that the evil enemy will not gain
power over me.
Amen.

—Martin Luther

Prayer is the spirit speaking truth to Truth.

—Philip James Bailey

The sacrifice of the wicked is an abomination to the LORD, But the prayer of the upright is His delight.
—Proverbs 15:8

November

By reflection and prayer, by reading and meditation, we can make our hearts a place where a blessing of peace would desire to abide.

—Edward Hays

May my prayer be set before you like incense;
may the lifting up of my hands be like the
evening sacrifice.
—Psalm 141:2 NIV

We reach a new plateau in our Christian faith and discover a new aspect of God's omnipotence on our behalf when we learn to trust Him with unanswered prayer and to thank Him for what His love denies.

—Robert J. Morgan

The Lord's Prayer contains the sum total of religion and morals.

—Duke of Wellington

Brethren, pray for us.
—1 Thessalonians 5:25

Prayer is not only asking, but an attitude of mind which produces the atmosphere in which asking is perfectly natural.

—Oswald Chambers

11 November

Lord! thou knowest how busy I must be this day:
if I forget thee, do not thou forget me.

—Sir Jacob Astley

My eyes are awake through the night watches,
That I may meditate on Your word.
—Psalm 119:148

Prayer is the highest use to which speech can be put. It is the highest meaning that can be put into words. Indeed, it breaks through language and escapes into action. We could never be told of what passed in Christ's mountain midnights. Words fail us in prayer oftener than anywhere else; and the Spirit must come in aid of our infirmity, set out our case to God, and give to us an unspoken freedom in prayer, the possession of our central soul, the reality of our inmost personality in organic contact with His.

—P. T. Forsyth

When we pray for the Spirit's help, it will no longer be in the fear that prayer is too great an effort for us. Instead, we will simply fall down at the Lord's feet in our weakness. There we will find the victory and power that comes from His love.

—Andrew Murray

*Sometimes the most important thing in a whole day
is the rest we take between two deep breaths,
or the turning inwards in prayer for five short minutes.*

— Etty Hillesum

*We give thanks to the God and Father of our
Lord Jesus Christ, praying always for you.*
—Colossians 1:3

*Take God for your spouse and friend and walk
with him continually, and you will not sin and will
learn to love, and the things you must do
will work out prosperously for you.*

— **St. John of the Cross**

We need never shout across the spaces to an absent God. He is nearer than our own soul, closer than our most secret thoughts.

—A. W. Tozer

Night and day we pray earnestly for you, asking God to let us see you again to fill up anything that may still be missing in your faith.
—1 Thessalonians 3:10 NLT

Prayer isn't magic. Jesus did not come to make our suffering disappear in an instant. Instead he came to fill it with His presence.

—Barbara Johnson

Don't put people down, unless it's on your prayer list.

—Stan Michalski

I will praise You, O LORD, with my whole heart; I will tell of all Your marvelous works.
—Psalm 9:1

How vast are the possibilities of prayer! How wide is its reach! What great things are accomplished by this divinely appointed means of grace! It lays its hand on Almighty God and moves Him to do what He would not otherwise do if prayer was not offered. It brings things to pass which would never otherwise occur. The story of prayer is the story of great achievements. Prayer is a wonderful power placed by Almighty God in the hands of His saints, which may be used to accomplish great purposes and to achieve unusual results. Prayer reaches to everything, takes in all things great and small which are promised by God to the children of men.

—E. M. Bounds

*Practice in life whatever you pray for and
God will give it to you more abundantly.*

— Edward Bouverie Pusey

*Now I beg you, brethren, through the Lord
Jesus Christ, and through the love of the
Spirit, that you strive together with me in
prayers to God for me.*
—Romans 15:30

21 November

It is from prayer that the spirit's victory springs.

—Schillerbuch

Prayer should be short, without giving God Almighty reasons why he should grant this or that; he knows best what is good for us.

—John Selden

Look to the LORD and his strength; seek his face always.
—1 Chronicles 16:11 NIV

Hasten therefore to share in the Holy Spirit. He is with you when you call upon Him; you can call upon Him only because He is already present. When He comes in answer to your prayer, He comes with an abundance of blessings. He is the river whose streams give joy to the city of God.

—**William of St. Thierry**

Do not make prayer a monologue—make it a conversation.

—Unknown

O Lord, You have heard the desire of the humble; You will strengthen their heart, You will incline Your ear.
—Psalm 10:17 NASB

We turn to God for help when our foundations are shaking, only to learn that it is God who is shaking them.

—**Charles C. West**

I will look to the LORD; I will wait for the God of my salvation; My God will hear me.
—**Micah 7:7**

Prayer has its great end when it lifts us to be more conscious and more sure of the gift than the need, of the grace than the sin. As petition rises out of need or sin, in our first prayer it comes first; but it may fall into a subordinate place when, at the end and height of our worship, we are filled with the fullness of God. "In that day ye shall ask Me nothing." Inward sorrow is fulfilled in the prayer of petition; inward joy in the prayer of thanksgiving. And this thought helps to deal with the question as to the hearing of prayer, and especially its answer. Or rather as to the place and kind of answer. We shall come one day to a heaven where we shall gratefully know that God's great refusals were sometimes the true answers to our truest prayer. Our soul is fulfilled if our petition is not.

—P. T. Forsyth

27 November

*Prayer is less about changing the world
than it is about changing ourselves.*

—**David J. Wolpe**

A generous prayer is never presented in vain; the petition may be refused, but the petitioner is always, I believe, rewarded by some gracious visitation.

—Robert Louis Stevenson

In my distress I called upon the LORD, And cried out to my God; He heard my voice from His temple, And my cry came before Him, even to His ears.
—Psalm 18:6

November

Every evening I turn my worries over to God.
He's going to be up all night anyway.

—Mary C. Crowley

Prayer and love are learned in the hour when prayer becomes impossible and your heart has turned to stone.

—Thomas Merton

This kind does not go out except by prayer and fasting.
—Matthew 17:21

December

God understands our prayers even when
we can't find the words to say them.

—Unknown

Some of God's greatest gifts are unanswered prayers.

—Garth Brooks

He fulfills the desires of those who fear him;
he hears their cry and saves them.
—Psalm 145:19 NIV

Psalm 5

Give ear to my words, O Lord,
consider my sighing.
Listen to my cry for help,
my King and my God,
for to you I pray.
In the morning, O Lord, you hear
my voice;
in the morning I lay my requests
before you
and wait in expectation. . . .

But I, by your great mercy,
will come into your house;
in reverence will I bow down
toward your holy temple. . . .

But let all who take refuge in you
be glad;
let them ever sing for joy.
Spread your protection over them,
that those who love your name
may rejoice in you.
For surely, O Lord, you bless
the righteous;
you surround them with your favor
as with a shield.

—Psalm 5:1–3, 7, 11–12, niv

Think positively about yourself, keep your thoughts and your actions clean, ask God who made you to keep on remaking you.

—Norman Vincent Peale

Jesus the Son of God, let us hold firmly to the faith we profess.
—Hebrews 4:14

We should always pray with as much earnestness as those who expect everything from God; we should always act with as much energy as those who expect everything from themselves.

—Charles C. Colson

If you abide in Me, and My words abide in you, you will ask what you desire, and it shall be done for you.

—John 15:7

Wherever . . . thou shalt be, pray secretly within thyself. If thou shalt be far from a house of prayer, give not thyself trouble to seek for one, for thou thyself art a sanctuary designed for prayer. If thou shalt be in bed, or in any other place, pray there; thy temple is there.

—**Bernard of Clairveaux**

December

If the Lord be with us, we have no cause of fear. His eye is upon us, His arm over us, His ear open to our prayer—His grace sufficient, His promises unchangeable.

—John Newton

I have no doubt that the world stands because of the prayer of Christians.

—Aristedes of Athens

They will call on My name, And I will answer them. I will say, "This is My people"; And each one will say, "The LORD is my God."
—Zechariah 13:9

The mind is not perfectly at prayer until the one praying does not think of himself or know he is praying.

—Antony of Egypt

This Book of the Law shall not depart from your mouth, but you shall meditate in it day and night.
—Joshua 1:8

You can bring your daily cares and needs to God in prayer any time, any place. He is intimately interested in the details of your life. You can ask for His guidance in your relationships, for help in whatever you need, for provision for financial and physical needs. Prayer does not have to be elaborate or long. A quick prayer as you bandage skinned knees or cook dinner connects you with your heavenly Father in an instant. He loves your heartfelt prayers, whether you need to pray in church or sing worship songs as you go about your daily work.

Prayer is communion with the God who loves you. You can cultivate many forms of prayer: praise worship, thanksgiving, confession, adoration, petition, supplication, intercession, and meditative prayer. When you pray you come into God's presence and discover that God has been present with you all along.

—Checklist for Life for Women

Ask God to fit you with His armor when you pray. Trust the Lord to guard your time with Him. If you fail, don't be depressed. God still waits for you. The victory in the battle of prayer is yours.

—Charles Stanley

As I urged you above, the moment you start praying, raising your heart upwards, and lower your eyes downwards; enter inside your inner person and pray in secret to your Father in heaven.

—**Aphrahat**

Hasten, O God, to save me; O LORD, come quickly to help me.
—**Psalm 70:1** NIV

13 December

At a time when you are in trouble, offer up petition, and when you are well supplied with good things, you should give thanks to the Giver, and when your mind rejoices, offer up praise.

—Aphrahat

Trouble and perplexity drive us to prayer, and
prayer driveth away trouble and perplexity.

—**Philipp Melanchthon**

*I pray, L*ORD *God of heaven, O great and*
awesome God, You who keep Your covenant
and mercy with those who love You.
—**Nehemiah 1:5**

It all starts with prayer. If you are not praying then it isn't going to start with you.

—Craig Riggle

Blessed is the person who has consented to become the close friend of faith and of prayer; he lives in singlemindedness and makes prayer and faith stop by with him.

—Ephraem the Syrian

Fix your thoughts on what is true and honorable and right. Think about things that are pure and lovely and admirable. Think about things that are excellent and worthy of praise.
—Philippians 4:8 NLT

JUST FOR TODAY

Lord, for tomorrow and its
needs I do not pray;
Keep me, my God, from
stain of sin just for today.
Help me to labor earnestly
and duly pray;
Let me be kind in word and
deed, Father, today.

Let me no wrong or idle
word unthinking say;
Set Thou a seal upon my lips
through all today.
Let me in season, Lord, be
grave, in season gay;
Let me be faithful to Thy
grace, dear Lord, today.

And if, today, this life of
mine should ebb away,
Give me Thy sacrament
divine, Father, today.
So for tomorrow and its
needs I do not pray;
Still keep me, guide me, love
me, Lord, through each day.

—Sybil F. Partridge

Set off on the path of prayer with confidence, then swiftly and speedily will you reach the place of peace, which is your stronghold against the place of fear.

—Evagrius of Pontus

Prayer also will be made for Him continually, And daily He shall be praised.
—Psalm 72:15

All I know is that when I pray, coincidences happen; and when I don't pray, they don't happen.

—**Sir William Temple**

Make it the first daily business to understand some part of the Bible clearly, and then the rest of the day to obey it.

—John Ruskin

Meditate on these things; give yourself entirely to them.
—1 Timothy 4:15

If you pray truly, you will feel within yourself a great assurance; and the angels will be your companions.

—Evagrius of Pontus

Hear in heaven their prayer and their supplication, and maintain their cause.
—1 Kings 8:45

Wash your face every morning in a bath of praise.

—**Charles Haddon Spurgeon**

To pray is to change. Prayer is the central avenue
God uses to transform us.

—Richard Foster

Please, LORD, please save us. Please, LORD,
please give us success.
—Psalm 118:25

Prayer wings its way from our lips and hearts through the heavens to the very Throne Room of God Himself. Prayer is a commanded activity. God tells us to pray, and He promises to hear and to heed; He promises to move heaven and earth to answer our prayers.

Of course, God does hear every prayer in a literal sense. He is omniscient and He is omnipresent. Now a sparrow falls to the ground without His notice. He hears every sound in the entire universe. He is ignorant of nothing.

God can do great things. He can perform miracles in our lives. He longs to hear and to answer prayer. His hand is strong enough to accomplish what is needed, and His ear is sharp enough to hear the faintest cry.

There are certain needs in our lives that can only be met through prayer. There are certain things in this world that can only be done through prayer. We have never stood in greater need of prayer. In our lives, and in the life of our nation and of our world, we need to have power with God and man. We need to be able to draw down from heaven a revival for our generation. We need to move heaven and earth through the power of prayer.

—Robert J. Morgan

There is no need to talk a lot in prayer, but stretch out your hands often and say, 'Lord, as you want and as you know, have mercy on me.'
But if there is war in your soul, add, 'Help me."
And because He knows what we need, He shows us His mercy.

—Macarius the Elder

If a man's deeds are not in harmony with his prayer,
he labours in vain.

—Moses

Please, LORD, please save us. Please, LORD,
please give us success.
—Psalm 118:25 NLT

At the times when you remember God, increase your prayers, so that when you forget him, the Lord may remind you.

—Mark the Ascetic

Give thanks to the LORD, for his love endures forever.
—2 Chronicles 20:21 NIV

When we are linked by the power of prayer, we hold each other's hand, as it were, while we walk along a slippery path; and so by the generous bounty of charity it comes about that the harder each one leans on the other, the more firmly we are bonded together in brotherly love.

—Gregory the Great

If God is slow in answering your request, and you ask but do not promptly receive anything, do not be upset, for you are not wiser than God.

—Abraham of Nathpar

Prayer is not just coming to Jesus; it is letting Jesus come into me.

—Becky Tirabassi

Accept my offerings of praise and teach me your laws.
—Psalm 119:108 CEV

Wandering is good when the mind wanders on God during the entire extent of one's prayer.

—Abraham of Nathpar

May my meditation be sweet to Him; I will be glad in the LORD.
—Psalm 104:34

Acknowledgments

Grateful acknowledgment is made to the following for permission to reprint copyrighted material:

Adventurous Prayer © 2003, excerpted by permission of Thomas Nelson Publishers.

Checklist for Life© 2002 GRQ, Inc., excerpted by permission of Thomas Nelson Publishers.

Donelson Fellowship, The ©2004, *Pocket Papers, http://www.donelson.org/pocket.cfm.*

Barbara Johnson, excerpted by permission of W Publishing Group, a division of Thomas Nelson Publishers from the book entitled *The Great Adventure* © 2002.

—*Devotions for a Sensational Life* © 2002, excerpted by permission of Thomas Nelson Publishers.

—*Daily Splashes of Joy* © 2000, excerpted by permission of W Publishing Group, a division of Thomas Nelson Publishers.

Nicole Johnson, excerpted by permission of W Publishing Group, a division of Thomas Nelson Publishers from the book entitled *Irrepressible Hope* © 2002.

Anne Graham Lotz, excerpted by permission of W Publishing Group, a division of Thomas Nelson Publishers from the book entitled *Just Give Me Jesus* © 2003 by Anne Graham Lotz.

Max Lucado, excerpted by permission of J. Countryman, a division of Thomas Nelson Publishers from the book entitled *Grace for the Moment* © 2002.

Catherine Marshall, excerpted by permission of J. Countryman, a division of Thomas Nelson Publishers from the book entitled Moments That Matter © 2001 by Marshall-LeSourd LLC.

John C. Maxwell, excerpted by permission of J. Countryman, a division of Thomas Nelson Publishers from the book entitled Leadership© 2001 by John C. Maxwell.

Stormie Omartian, excerpted by permission of Thomas Nelson Publishers from the book entitled Lord I Want to be Whole © 2001 by Stormie Omartian.

—*Praying God's Will for Your Life,* © 2001 by Stormie Omartian.

Luci Swindoll, excerpted by permission of W Publishing Group, a division of Thomas Nelson Publishers from the book entitled *The Great Adventure* © 2002.

—*Devotions for a Sensational Life* © 2002, excerpted by permission of Thomas Nelson Publishers.

—*You Bring the Confetti, God Brings the Joy* © 1997, excerpted by permission of W Publishing Group, a division of Thomas Nelson Publishers.

Charles Stanley, excerpted by permission of Thomas Nelson Publishers from the book entitled *On Holy Ground* © 1999 by Charles Stanley.

—Into His Presence, © 2000 by Charles Stanley, excerpted by permission of Thomas Nelson Publishers.

Penelope J. Stokes, excerpted by permission of J. Countryman, a division of Thomas Nelson Publishers from the book entitled Beside A Quiet Stream © 1999 by Penelope J. Stokes.

Becky Tirabassi, excerpted by permission of Thomas Nelson Publishers from the book entitled *Let Prayer Change Your Life* © 1990, 1992, 2000 by Becky Tirabassi.

Sheila Walsh, excerpted by permission of W Publishing Group Thomas Nelson Publishers from the book entitled *The Great Adventure* © 2002

Prayer Requests

Prayer Requests

Prayer Requests

Prayer Requests

Prayers Answered

Prayers Answered

Scriptures to Read and Remember

Scriptures to Read and Remember